LEWES

THEN and NOW – Volume 2

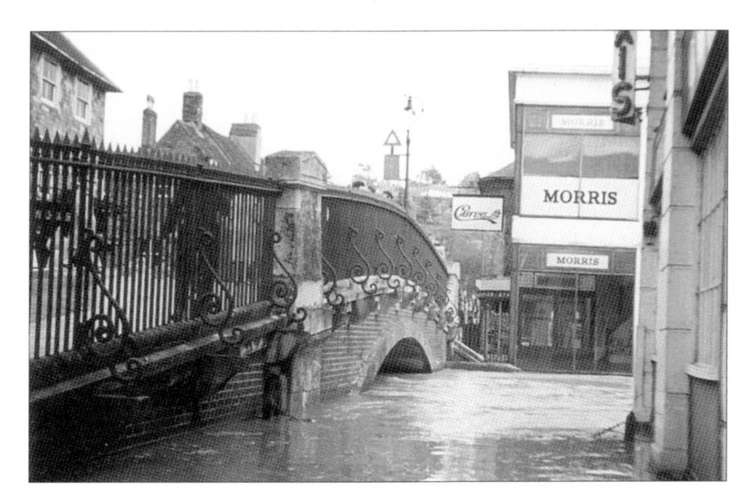

Bill Young
in association with David Arscott

S. B. Publications

Previous titles by Bill Young
Line of Fire – A History of Firefighting in Lewes (1996)
Lewes Then and Now (1998) (In association with Bob Cairns)

First published in 2004 by S B Publications
19 Grove Road, Seaford, Sussex BN25 1TP

ISBN 1-85770-287-5

Typeset by D.Arscott at
Pomegranate Press

Printed by
Pageturn Ltd, Hove. BN3 7DX
01273 821500

Preface

This book was in preparation when Bill Young died. As with his first volume, the idea was to contrast photographs of today with those showing Lewes as it was in the past. One difference, apart from the areas selected, was that on this occasion most of the 'yesterday' views would be within the living memory of many Lewesians – chiefly, although not exclusively, images from the 1950s to the 1970s. Another was that Bill wished to include, however briefly, the recollections of some of those who remembered places now so changed as to be barely recognisable, and he had gathered a sheaf of such memories in preparation. Those who helped him in this way – and others whose help has been enlisted more recently – are thanked on page 96.

Doubtless Bill's final decisions about what to include and what to leave out would have produced a slightly different volume, but I very much hope that this tribute to our county town will also be seen as a fitting tribute to the man himself.

David Arscott

Cozy Cafe, Malling Street, 1972. The original entrance to the Cuilfail estate lay just beyond the three-storey building on the right.

FRIAR'S WALK, 1967. The old station is in the process of being pulled down.
"My grandfather was a signalman on the railways, and my grandparents used to live in the Old Station House, as did my mother and her sister. They took in as a lodger the man who subsequently married my mother. The railway ran at the back of Old Station House garden, and as children they used to run out and wave to the people in trains on the embankment above. It was a bit like 'The Railway Children', I suppose."

NOW: The magistrates' court occupies the site of the former station, which leaves not a trace behind. Many regard the destruction of the Lewes–Uckfield line as a bad mistake, and there is a campaign to have it restored.

WHARFS BY THE OUSE FROM CLIFFE BRIDGE DURING THE 1960 FLOODS.

"Before the building of Phoenix Causeway, to get to work at Caffyns I would have to cycle down Cliffe High Street and along Malling Street. During the early part of the war the Bailey bridge provided a short cut to work."

"Barges would come up the Ouse to the iron works and to Parsons' timber yard. I seem to recall the barges getting stuck underneath Cliffe Bridge."

NOW: The Phoenix Causeway – the first stage of what would have been a dramatic and disfiguring inner relief road – straddles the river at this point. During 2000 there was further serious flooding, leaving hundreds of people homeless, some of them for more than two years.

OFF EASTGATE STREET.

"Mansfield's Garage, Caffyns' big rivals and Vauxhall main dealers, had premises down here until their new buildings were erected in Spital Road."

"I remember that it was a difficult business getting the huge concrete beams down this lane for the part of the Phoenix Causeway bridge that was built on that side of the river."

NOW: The line of supermarket trolleys reveals that this is the area in front of Safeway's today. An unlikely survivor of the restructuring of this area is the large chestnut tree outside the store, whose leaves can be seen at the far left of the photograph.

BRIDGMAN'S, EASTGATE STREET, 1966.

"I can remember going into the mason's yard and watching the stone being cut by huge (or so they seemed to us youngsters) bow saws."

"The dad of one of my school mates worked here – Mr Hills. He let me bore a hole in a piece of stone."

NOW: The houses behind have all gone, removed for road widening, but Bridgman's has managed to survive.

COTTAGES AND BAPTIST CHURCH HALL IN EASTGATE STREET.

"As children roaming the streets, as we could safely do in those days, we used to call at one of these little houses in the knowledge that the old lady who lived there would come out and bring us sweets or a cold drink."

"The front was covered in Virginia creeper, and the reds of the leaves in autumn were a sight to see as you turned the corner from Little East Street."

NOW: Another part of the Lewes townscape which has succumbed to the demands of the car.

LITTLE EAST STREET.

"I remember going to events at Eastgate Baptist church hall. There were six rooms and the large hall. One of my earliest memories is its mustiness. The church hosted a Women's Hour there, a hundred strong, and there was a Boys' Brigade and a Girls' Life Brigade."

NOW: The buildings this side of Waterloo Place have been swept away, and the road has become a busy thoroughfare.
"We used to call the hill in the background 'Fat belly woman'. We would go grass sledging on the slopes. The small sledges had wooden runners, and we lubricated them with paraffin that we carried with us in a small bottle and applied with a piece of rag. It made the sledges move pretty fast"

THE UCKFIELD LINE RAILWAY BRIDGE FROM SCHOOL HILL.

"Traffic was two-way in those days. I managed to free-wheel on my bicycle from the War Memorial to just over Cliffe Bridge – but I had to make sure the traffic lights were at green!"
"I've seen buses stuck under this bridge. Joe Light, a scrap merchant, bought a lot of redundant trolley buses from Brighton Corporation. He brought the first one through Lewes on tow, but when he got to the bridge the 'arms' wouldn't go under it, and he had to find another route."

NOW: The foreground is much the same, but there's a pedestrian precinct at the foot of School Hill, leading towards Cliffe Bridge. The Gourmet delicatessen occupied the shop with the bow window on the right before it was taken over by Pizza Express. Before that it housed the office of the builders, C.J. Pannett.

FITZROY HOUSE, 1970.

"The little shop on the side of Fitzroy House, which later belonged to Hunts, was once Urrys fuel order office. You could buy a sack or two of coal from the yard."

NOW: Fitzroy House, originally built as a library, is today in private hands.

FLUDES.

"This was the Seveirg building, and most of it had been converted to flats by this time. Before Fludes it was Redhill Motors."

"Just to the right of this building was a butcher's shop, Chas. Colbourne."

NOW: Boots the Chemist occupies the former Fludes corner site.

APPROACH TO CLIFFE BRIDGE.

"Before the railway bridge was demolished and new, higher buses appeared, the road had to be scraped and lowered so that buses could pass under it."
"Mansfield's Garage had its showrooms just east of the dismantled bridge, and also close by was Langham Continental, a classy ladies' outfitters."

NOW: A modern development of shops occupies most of the site, which is a pedestrian precinct.

CLIFFE HIGH STREET, 1960.

"The little supermarket on the corner of the High Street and Bear Yard was a Victor Value store, and then a Tesco's."

"The first shop on the left, just over the old bridge, was the Bazaar. Next was Wilmshurst's the fruiterers and greengrocers, and then Harvey's and Hepworth's. Halfway down is the neon sign of the Polar Bear milk bar."

NOW: Harvey's shop has expanded towards the bridge on the far side of the street. On this side, the Argos building, formerly Caffyns, stands on the site of the former Bear Inn, burned down in Victorian times. Bill's Produce Store occupies the corner of Cliffe High Street and Bear Lane.

ODEON CINEMA, CLIFFE HIGH STREET.

"On the left-hand side of the Odeon, at no. 33, was J.B. Bennett & Co, the ironmongers. I believe the porched entrance next to it was a school in earlier days. On the other side of the cinema was the 'Q' library."

NOW: Lewes has no cinema today. The Odeon has been replaced by small shops and a walkway – largely built on the former cinema site – through to South Cliffe.

ST THOMAS CHURCH, CLIFFE CORNER.

"I believe that the butchers by the church was Watford's, with Shaw's the grocers standing on the corner."

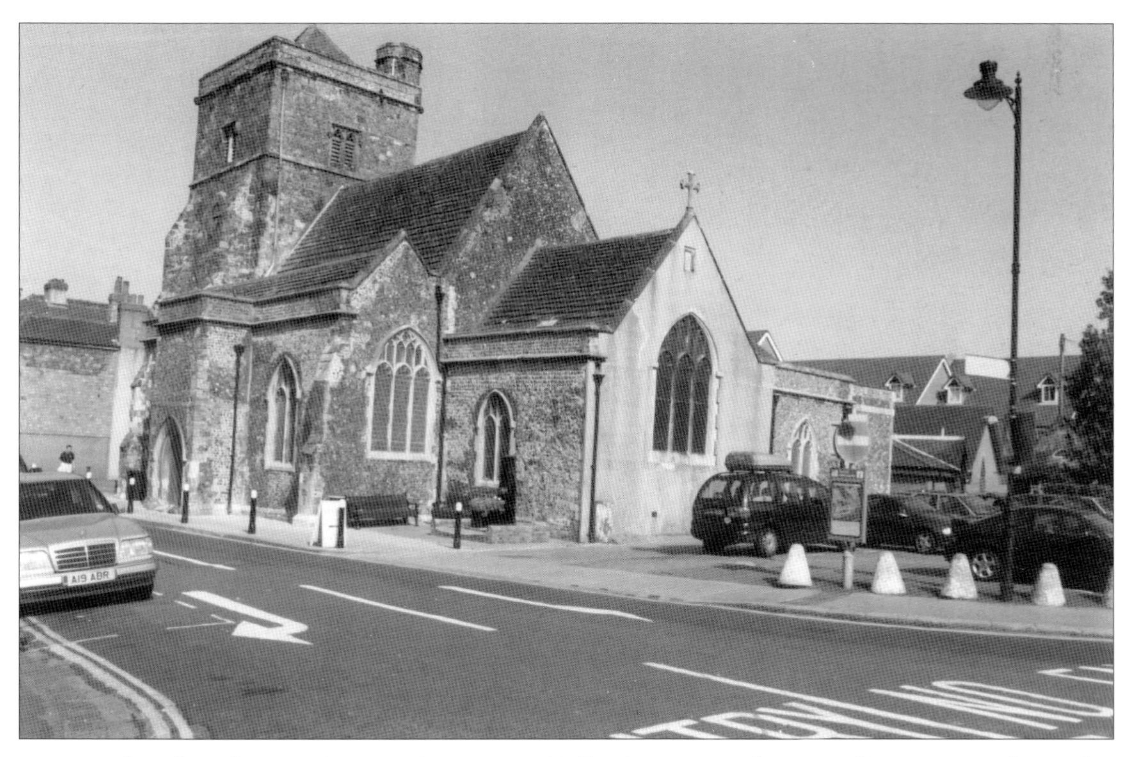

NOW: The church stands in isolation on Cliffe Corner, with a small car park where the demolished buildings once stood. The 'sharks' teeth' bollards are anti-tank obstructions from the second world war.

SOUTH STREET.

'Heavy lorries from the cement works and from the continent – an absolute nightmare!"

NOW: The building of the Cuilfail Tunnel has allowed South Street, once a major thoroughfare in and out of the town, to become a cul-de-sac in which it is rather more safe to ride a bicycle.

MALLING STREET / SOUTH STREET.

"The newsagents shop here was Jenkins and Stripp, later R & J Ellis. I did rounds for them, along the length of Malling Street and over to the Deanery next to South Malling church."
"George Ranscombe, who ran the Dorset Arms, kept pigs and chickens in his yard."

NOW: A swathe of buildings has come down in front of the Dorset Arms to make way for a new road system which involved changing the point of entry to the Cuilfail estate up on the hill.

MALLING STREET, EAST SIDE.

"That's the Melbourne Guest House with the hanging sign. It was no. 55. In the early 1940s I was a delivery boy for Hepworths, and the manager, a Mr Pringle, lodged there. It was my job to collect his tea-time sandwiches from the Melbourne and take them to the shop in Cliffe."
"The grey-fronted building was occupied by Mr and Mrs Russell of the shoe firm Russell & Bromley. Mother was in domestic service there."

NOW: The present two parts of Malling Street were once connected, and ran uninterupted into South Street. The buildings on the facing page stood somewhere close to today's tunnel mouth.

MALLING STREET, WEST SIDE.

"This was taken long before 1960, perhaps as early as 1940. You can see the Jireh Chapel gates at the far end of the street. Coming this way you have Soap Factory Lane and then Hoopers Lane under the Caffyns sign. The houses either side were requisitioned by the Canadian Military Police, many of whom didn't come back from the Dieppe Raid."

NOW: It's impossible to take the photograph on the facing page from the same place today, so this one – taken from the other direction – must suffice. The road continued north in a righthand curve, well in front of the end of Jireh Chapel, whose ornamental gate therefore fronted a long drive. The houses beyond it have all gone.

MALLING STREET.
"In the foreground is one of the two burial grounds for St Thomas's church."
"The clock over the bay window advertised William Weller the undertaker's."

NOW: The building on the right is the one in the same position on the photograph opposite. An undertaker's business still occupies the site next door, but the modern building is much less pleasing.

HOOPERS LANE IN THE 1960 FLOODS.
"This car, a Buick, belonged to a Mr Thornycroft and was the last vehicle to be towed out of the garage as the flood waters rose – by this time the water was up to our chests."
"During the war a Bailey bridge was erected at the end of Hoopers Lane, taking the line of the present Phoenix Causeway. The approach ran past the slaughter house and two cottages that can be seen in the photograph. Tanks rumbled across at all hours of the day and night."
"We used to buy meat for our dog from the slaughterhouse."

NOW: The buildings remain to remind us of a lane, close by the Phoenix Causeway, which has completely disappeared during road widening.

MALLING STREET, EAST SIDE 1972.

"This was all that remained of a former brewery, latterly used as a furniture depository. It was badly damaged in a fire."

NOW: Small commercial units occupy the site by the side of what is an increasingly busy road.

MALLING STREET, EAST SIDE.

"I grew up at no. 130 Malling Street and my husband at no. 134, and we now live at Malling Down – so we haven't moved very far!"

"The glass conservatory was part of Clayhill Nurseries, which went back a long way behind."

"The line of cottages was known as Tanner's Row."

NOW: The road has been slightly widened, and a small housing development, The Spinneys, has been erected on the site of the cottages and nursery.

APPLEYARD'S GARAGE, MALLING STREET.
"This was originally Twort's Garage."
"Appleyard's was a pretty busy place. They sold cars there as well as repairing them."

NOW: Nothing could match the character of the old garage with its aged petrol pumps, but a filling station remains on the site.

ORCHARD ROAD.

"The large house in the background was called the Grey House. It was owned by a Mr Gosling, who was a local councillor and had a shop in Cliffe High Street."
"At another time it was lived in by a mayor of Lewes, Mr Bennett, and his family."

NOW: The trees have grown, and the street has a comfortable suburban character.

NORTH STREET, WEST SIDE.
"These buildings were demolished after a bomb fell on the area during the last war."

NOW: Ugliness has replaced the attractive character of the former row of Georgian houses, the site occupied by a brutal telephone exchange.

NORTH STREET, EAST SIDE.

"Bill Tester, who had the house on the left with the ornate lamps above the door, had a coal merchant's yard just round the corner in Wellington Street."

"I believe these cottages were demolished for slum clearance. They were all individual – some brick, some weather-boarded."

NOW: Undifferentiated, and uncompromising, flats and maisonettes occupy the site.

NORTH STREET.

"The shop on the left was a grocer's, and the area round the corner on the left we used to call Tiger's Bay. The building at the end of the street was the fire station."

"We could play in the streets then. One winter I whizzed down the road on my ice skates."

NOW: The houses have been swept away from both sides of the street. The fire station remains, although it is no longer used for this purpose – modern premises were built to the left of it. A car and coach park have replaced the cottages on the left hand side, beyond Gorringe's auction house.

BOTTOM OF NORTH STREET, 1969.

"The white building, centre right, was part of Every's ironworks. It was at one time the largest employer in the town, with more staff than the county council."

"I remember my school organising a visit to the foundry and how fascinated I was by the casting pits. I especially enjoyed the pattern shop with its lovely workmanship."

NOW: The houses have been replaced by a garage on the corner of a road which leads to an industrial estate.

WELLINGTON MOTORS, WELLINGTON STREET, 1973.
"It was a small garage, but the VIP petrol was very cheap."
"The main rivals to Caffyns were Mansfield's. Wellington Motors weren't in the same league."

NOW: Motorists have to go elsewhere for their fuel today. The housing development seen on page 53 extends as far as this corner.

FLOODED RAILWAY GOODS LINES, 1960.

"You can see both Corrall's office and the repair depot for Post Office vehicles. The bridge led to allotments for railway workers. Burwood Godley, who owned Leighside, built the splendid house in the background for his gardener. It had an observatory, which Godley used himself."

NOW: Station car parking is more important for the railway today than a coal yard and goods lines.

LEWES RAILWAY STATION, 1960.

"The water flowing onto the track was from the Winterbourne Stream. As pressure build up behind the wall, engineers decided to punch a hole in it in order to release the pressure."

NOW: The station car park extends into an area once used as allotments.

LEWES CATTLE MARKET SITE DURING DEMOLITION.
"Monday was always market day, Sheep and cows were driven though the streets to Garden Street, where the market was held."
"On a Friday in the mid-1970s it became a general market selling produce, clothes etc. It closed in 1992."

NOW: A new housing estate, Tanners Brook, occupies most of the old market site.

BELL LANE SCENT FACTORY, 1973.

"If the wind was blowing in the wrong direction the smell from the factory reached Grange Road, where I lived."

"I remember delivering crates of lemonade to the top floor of this seven-storey building when it was owned by Gosnells."

NOW: A modern factory building has replaced the former brewery buildings. County Hall can be seen rearing up behind.

WINTERBOURNE FARM, BELL LANE, 1973.
"Thomas Fitton, who lived in the building that fronted the road, was a trainer at the stables at Winterbourne Farm in 1920."
"I remember the houses in Winterbourne Hollow being built between 1936 and 1939."

NOW: Most of the farm buildings are today part of Winterbourne Mews.

GARDEN STREET, 1960.

"I waded through the flood water in my wellingtons and turned right into the cattle market. There was a sign here that said: Cattle & calves turn right; pigs straight on."

NOW: The street has been 'traffic calmed' and, with the replacement of the market by the houses of Tanners Brook, retains its original character.

WESTGATE STREET.

"Mr Appleby ran a butcher's shop."

"The street used to be called White Lion Lane, after the pub of that name. It was pulled down for slum clearance in the 1930s, and the area's just a car park now."

NOW: The Full of Beans health food shop can be seen on the left of the photograph, while the former butcher's shop has become residential.

The buildings on the right in the old photograph were demolished to make a wider road. After many years as a plumbers' merchant, the premises were taken over by the former Cadecraft shop. Today they house the Circa restaurant.

THE OLD MALTHOUSE, CASTLE PRECINCTS, 1973

"I remember that Beard's Brewery used this building for many years. It was originally built for the Castle Brewery in the 1850s."

NOW: With a new front door and altered windows, the Maltings houses the East Sussex county records office.

CASTLE DITCH LANE,
1973.

"The brewery building was Beard's. Further along the lane was the back entrance to the courts – it's sobering to think that many infamous criminals would have used this lane under guard."
"My uncle, Charlie Gearing, who took over the business of Mr Muddle, had a workshop up the passage where he made the coffins for his undertaker's business."

NOW: The chimney has gone. The buildings on the right have been tastefully converted for residential use, while those on the left house small businesses.

LANCASTER STREET, 1973.
"Just past the block of four houses was Mrs Bentley's shop. She mainly sold sweets, but also stocked some groceries."

NOW: A row of maisonettes occupies the site of the former cottages.

NEW STREET, 1970.

"On the left is the roof of Broad's candle factory, which later became Everett's hypodermic needle factory. The upstairs room next to the Crown Shades (in the background) was used by the Lewes Rifle Volunteer Club."

NOW: The terrace has gone – to be replaced, of course, by car parking. The industrial buildings are now home to a variety of craft shops.

WESTERN ROAD SCHOOL.

"One of my earliest recollections is watching a boy climb onto the roof and fall through the glass conservatory. The outside toilets used to freeze every winter, giving us days off school. When coke was delivered, we boys would use our own shovels and buckets to cart it round to the boiler house."

"My eldest son 'preached the gospel' to his classmates, and we were summoned to the head."

NOW: The primary school moved to the former Lewes Girls' Grammar School site in Southover. Today the buildings are used as a day centre for adults with special needs.

LEWES PRISON.
"The prefabs were erected during the war and housed prison officers and other staff. My father was a physical training instructor at the prison, and he and my mum lived in one of them for a time."

NOW: Car parking for prison staff occupies the site today.

NEW BRIDGE, JUGGS LANE.
"I remember that the arch of the bridge was built first, and the chalk was dug out beneath it."
"My wife's brother drove a lorry for Eastwood's Cement Works, and in this picture you can see that the business was still in production."

NOW: Vegetation has grown on top of the cutting, but its side still remains quite bare.

CRANEDOWN.

"There were allotments on the righthand side of the road, now of course covered by chalk."
"There was a water pumping station on the right, originally Lewes Water Co., but that has gone now."

NOW: The road has been moved to the left in order to bridge the bypass.

LEWES BYPASS.

"On the day that I took this photograph, my wife and I, together with two friends, walked the bypass from the Southerham roundabout."

"I remember doing 100mph in my Triumph Vitesse."

NOW: Bushes have grown to a good height on the right-hand side, but local residents nevertheless complain about the noise of traffic from the bypass.

TOLLHOUSE AND FOX INN, SOUTHERHAM.

"Both the Fox and the toll cottages were part of the Firle Estate. As an estate worker I occasionally quaffed a ginger beer and ate my sandwiches at the Fox. The road went on to Lewes via South Street."

NOW: The A27 passes above on a bridge, while the corner towards the hamlet of Southerham is neglected and strewn with litter.

WHITE BRIDGE, THE PELLS, 1964.
"I remember fishing for eels in the vicinity of the bridge. It was private, but it was opened to the public on Sundays so that people could attend South Malling church."
"I used to manage to overcome the obstacles, such as barbed wire, climb on to the bridge and jump up and down on it. Since it was a suspension bridge, this was great fun."

NOW: Today's photograph was taken from Willey's Bridge. Nothing remains of the old bridge but an anchorage point.

Acknowledgements

The publishers are grateful to all copyright holders who have given their permission for their images to be reproduced in this book, and will be pleased to correct any errors or omissions in future reprints. Thanks to Bob Davey (pages 40 and 60); Dorothy Eade (page 94); Roy Gear (pages 4, 10, 56, 58 and 78); Peter Hunt (front cover, frontispiece, pages 6, 12, 24, 48, 52, 62, 86, 88 and 90); Betty James (pages 28, 54 and 72); Peter Martin (pages 8, 14, 32, 34, 36, 44, 46, 82 and 84); Edward Reeves (page 50); East Sussex Library Service (preface and pages 16, 22, 66, 68, 74 and 76); National Monuments Record Centre (pages 18, 26 and 80); Sussex Archaeological Society (pages 3, 20, 38, 42, 64 , 70 and 92).

Several of Bill Young's friends and acquaintances kindly furnished him with their personal memories of the town, among them Ann Baldwin, Bob Baldwin, John Chaplin, Rita Chaplin, Jenny Clay, Shaun Clay, Bob Davey, Roy Geer, Ken Head, Peter Hunt, Ann Martin, Peter Martin, Jim Newell, Kath Price, Lesley Rooney, Charles Stephens and Simon Young.

Further thanks to Bob Towner, to John and Shirley Geering and to Robert Cheesman for their help in identifying and commenting upon areas of Lewes which have changed beyond recognition.